Year Month Name

Day	Date		TIME IN	TIME OUT	TOTAL h

D1733152

Year Month Name

Day	Date		TIME IN	TIME OUT	TOTAL h

Year Month Name

Day	Date		TIME IN	TIME OUT	TOTAL h

Year Month Name

Day	Date		TIME IN	TIME OUT	TOTAL h

Year Month Name

Day	Date		TIME IN	TIME OUT	TOTAL h

Year Month Name

Day	Date		TIME IN	TIME OUT	TOTAL h

Year Month Name

Day	Date		TIME IN	TIME OUT	TOTAL h

Year Month Name

Day	Date		TIME IN	TIME OUT	TOTAL h

Year Month Name

Day	Date		TIME IN	TIME OUT	TOTAL h

Year Month Name

Day	Date		TIME IN	TIME OUT	TOTAL h

Year Month Name

Day	Date		TIME IN	TIME OUT	TOTAL h

Year Month Name

Day	Date		TIME IN	TIME OUT	TOTAL h

Year Month Name

Day	Date		TIME IN	TIME OUT	TOTAL h

Year Month Name

Day	Date		TIME IN	TIME OUT	TOTAL h

Year Month Name

Day	Date		TIME IN	TIME OUT	TOTAL h

Year Month Name

Day	Date		TIME IN	TIME OUT	TOTAL h

Year Month Name

Day	Date		TIME IN	TIME OUT	TOTAL h

Year Month Name

Day	Date		TIME IN	TIME OUT	TOTAL h

Year Month Name

Day	Date		TIME IN	TIME OUT	TOTAL h

Year Month Name

Day	Date		TIME IN	TIME OUT	TOTAL h

Year Month Name

Day	Date		TIME IN	TIME OUT	TOTAL h

Year	Month	Name			
Day	Date		TIME IN	TIME OUT	TOTAL h

Year Month Name

Day	Date		TIME IN	TIME OUT	TOTAL h

Year Month Name

Day	Date		TIME IN	TIME OUT	TOTAL h

Year Month Name

Day	Date		TIME IN	TIME OUT	TOTAL h

Year Month Name

Day	Date		TIME IN	TIME OUT	TOTAL h

Year Month Name

Day	Date		TIME IN	TIME OUT	TOTAL h

Year Month Name

Day	Date		TIME IN	TIME OUT	TOTAL h

Year Month Name

Day	Date		TIME IN	TIME OUT	TOTAL h

Year Month Name

Day	Date		TIME IN	TIME OUT	TOTAL h

Year Month Name

Day	Date		TIME IN	TIME OUT	TOTAL h

Year Month Name

Day	Date		TIME IN	TIME OUT	TOTAL h

Year Month Name

Day	Date		TIME IN	TIME OUT	TOTAL h

Year Month Name

Day	Date		TIME IN	TIME OUT	TOTAL h

Year Month Name

Day	Date		TIME IN	TIME OUT	TOTAL h

Year Month Name

Day	Date		TIME IN	TIME OUT	TOTAL h

Year Month Name

Day	Date		TIME IN	TIME OUT	TOTAL h

Year Month Name

Day	Date		TIME IN	TIME OUT	TOTAL h

Year Month Name

Day	Date		TIME IN	TIME OUT	TOTAL h

Year Month Name

Day	Date		TIME IN	TIME OUT	TOTAL h

Year Month Name

Day	Date		TIME IN	TIME OUT	TOTAL h

Year Month Name

Day	Date		TIME IN	TIME OUT	TOTAL h

Year Month Name

Day	Date		TIME IN	TIME OUT	TOTAL h

Year Month Name

Day	Date		TIME IN	TIME OUT	TOTAL h

Year Month Name

Day	Date		TIME IN	TIME OUT	TOTAL h

Year Month Name

Day	Date		TIME IN	TIME OUT	TOTAL h

Year	Month	Name			
Day	Date		TIME IN	TIME OUT	TOTAL h

Year Month Name

Day	Date		TIME IN	TIME OUT	TOTAL h

Year Month Name

Day	Date		TIME IN	TIME OUT	TOTAL h

Year Month Name

Day	Date		TIME IN	TIME OUT	TOTAL h

Year Month Name

Day	Date		TIME IN	TIME OUT	TOTAL h

Year Month Name

Day	Date		TIME IN	TIME OUT	TOTAL h

Year Month Name

Day	Date		TIME IN	TIME OUT	TOTAL h

Year Month Name

Day	Date		TIME IN	TIME OUT	TOTAL h

Year Month Name

Day	Date		TIME IN	TIME OUT	TOTAL h

Year Month Name

Day	Date		TIME IN	TIME OUT	TOTAL h

Year Month Name

Day	Date		TIME IN	TIME OUT	TOTAL h

Year Month Name

Day	Date		TIME IN	TIME OUT	TOTAL h

Year Month Name

Day	Date		TIME IN	TIME OUT	TOTAL h

Year Month Name

Day	Date		TIME IN	TIME OUT	TOTAL h

Year Month Name

Day	Date		TIME IN	TIME OUT	TOTAL h

Year Month Name

Day	Date		TIME IN	TIME OUT	TOTAL h

Year Month Name

Day	Date		TIME IN	TIME OUT	TOTAL h

Year Month Name

Day	Date		TIME IN	TIME OUT	TOTAL h

Year Month Name

Day	Date		TIME IN	TIME OUT	TOTAL h

Year Month Name

Day	Date		TIME IN	TIME OUT	TOTAL h

Year	Month	Name			
Day	Date		TIME IN	TIME OUT	TOTAL h

Year Month Name

Day	Date		TIME IN	TIME OUT	TOTAL h

Year Month Name

Day	Date		TIME IN	TIME OUT	TOTAL h

Year Month Name

Day	Date		TIME IN	TIME OUT	TOTAL h

Year Month Name

Day	Date		TIME IN	TIME OUT	TOTAL h

Year Month Name

Day	Date		TIME IN	TIME OUT	TOTAL h

Year	Month	Name			
Day	Date		TIME IN	TIME OUT	TOTAL h

Year Month Name

Day	Date		TIME IN	TIME OUT	TOTAL h

Year Month Name

Day	Date		TIME IN	TIME OUT	TOTAL h

Year Month Name

Day	Date		TIME IN	TIME OUT	TOTAL h

Year Month Name

Day	Date		TIME IN	TIME OUT	TOTAL h

Year Month Name

Day	Date		TIME IN	TIME OUT	TOTAL h

Year Month Name

Day	Date		TIME IN	TIME OUT	TOTAL h

Year Month Name

Day	Date		TIME IN	TIME OUT	TOTAL h

Year Month Name

Day	Date		TIME IN	TIME OUT	TOTAL h

Year Month Name

Day	Date		TIME IN	TIME OUT	TOTAL h

Year Month Name

Day	Date		TIME IN	TIME OUT	TOTAL h

Year Month Name

Day	Date		TIME IN	TIME OUT	TOTAL h

Year	Month	Name			
Day	Date		TIME IN	TIME OUT	TOTAL h

Year Month Name

Day	Date		TIME IN	TIME OUT	TOTAL h

Year Month Name

Day	Date		TIME IN	TIME OUT	TOTAL h

Year Month Name

Day	Date		TIME IN	TIME OUT	TOTAL h

Year Month Name

Day	Date		TIME IN	TIME OUT	TOTAL h

Year Month Name

Day	Date		TIME IN	TIME OUT	TOTAL h

Year Month Name

Day	Date		TIME IN	TIME OUT	TOTAL h

Year Month Name

Day	Date		TIME IN	TIME OUT	TOTAL h

Year Month Name

Day	Date		TIME IN	TIME OUT	TOTAL h

Year Month Name

Day	Date		TIME IN	TIME OUT	TOTAL h

Year Month Name

Day	Date		TIME IN	TIME OUT	TOTAL h

Year Month Name

Day	Date		TIME IN	TIME OUT	TOTAL h

Year Month Name

Day	Date		TIME IN	TIME OUT	TOTAL h

Year Month Name

Day	Date		TIME IN	TIME OUT	TOTAL h

Year Month Name

Day	Date		TIME IN	TIME OUT	TOTAL h

Year Month Name

Day	Date		TIME IN	TIME OUT	TOTAL h

Year Month Name

Day	Date		TIME IN	TIME OUT	TOTAL h

Year Month Name

Day	Date		TIME IN	TIME OUT	TOTAL h

Year Month Name

Day	Date		TIME IN	TIME OUT	TOTAL h

Year Month Name

Day	Date		TIME IN	TIME OUT	TOTAL h

Year Month Name

Day	Date		TIME IN	TIME OUT	TOTAL h

Year Month Name

Day	Date		TIME IN	TIME OUT	TOTAL h

Year Month Name

Day	Date		TIME IN	TIME OUT	TOTAL h

Year Month Name

Day	Date		TIME IN	TIME OUT	TOTAL h

Year Month Name

Day	Date		TIME IN	TIME OUT	TOTAL h

Year Month Name

Day	Date		TIME IN	TIME OUT	TOTAL h

Made in the USA
Las Vegas, NV
05 November 2020

10586662R10061